The
UNITED STATES
PRESIDENTS

Chester
ARTHUR

Heidi M.D. Elston

Big Buddy Books

An Imprint of Abdo Publishing
abdopublishing.com

abdopublishing.com

Published by Abdo Publishing, a division of ABDO, PO Box 398166, Minneapolis, Minnesota 55439.
Copyright © 2017 by Abdo Consulting Group, Inc. International copyrights reserved in all countries. No
part of this book may be reproduced in any form without written permission from the publisher. Big Buddy
Books™ is a trademark and logo of Abdo Publishing.

Printed in the United States of America, North Mankato, Minnesota
062016
092016

THIS BOOK CONTAINS
RECYCLED MATERIALS

Design: Sarah DeYoung, Mighty Media, Inc.
Production: Mighty Media, Inc.
Editor: Rebecca Felix
Cover Photograph: Corbis
Interior Photographs: Alamy (p. 29); AP Images (pp. 7, 11); Corbis (pp. 19, 25); Getty Images (p. 5);
    Library of Congress (p. 6); National Archives (pp. 13, 15, 17); North Wind (p. 6);
    Picture History (pp. 9, 13, 21, 23, 27)

Cataloging-in-Publication Data

Names: Elston, Heidi M.D., author.
Title: Chester Arthur / by Heidi M.D. Elston.
Description: Minneapolis, MN : Abdo Publishing, [2017] | Series: United States
    presidents | Includes bibliographical references and index.
Identifiers: LCCN 2015044096 | ISBN 9781680780833 (lib. bdg.) |
    ISBN 9781680775037 (ebook)
Subjects: LCSH: Arthur, Chester, 1829-1886- --Juvenile literature. 2. Presidents-
    -United States--Biography--Juvenile literature. | United States--
    Politics and Government--1881-1885--Juvenile literature.
Classification: DDC 973.8/4092092 [B]--dc23
LC record available at http://lccn.loc.gov/2015044096

Contents

Chester Arthur

Chester Arthur was the twenty-first president of the United States. Before he was president, Arthur worked as a **lawyer**. He became vice president in March 1881.

On September 19, 1881, Arthur received shocking news. Around midnight, he learned President James A. Garfield had died. Arthur became president. He took the **oath** of office on September 20.

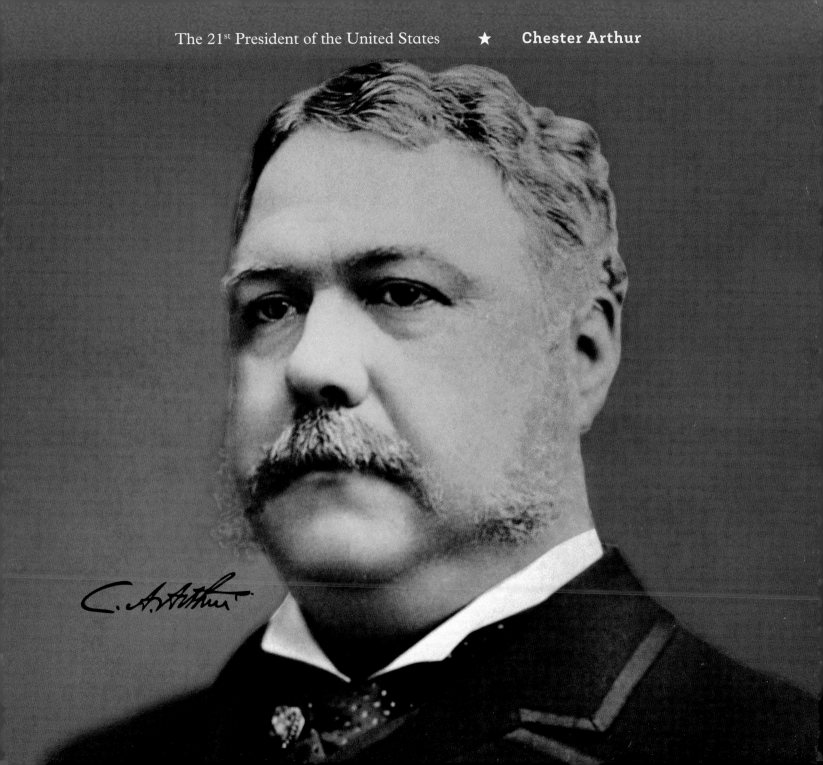

Timeline

1829

On October 5, Chester Alan Arthur was born in Fairfield, Vermont.

1859

On October 25, Arthur married Ellen Lewis Herndon.

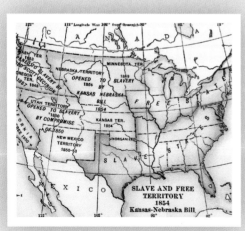

1854

Arthur became a **lawyer**.

1861

The **American Civil War** began. New York governor Edwin D. Morgan made Arthur New York quartermaster general.

1883

Arthur signed the Pendleton **Civil Service** Act.

1881

Arthur became James A. Garfield's vice president on March 4. On July 2, Garfield was shot. Garfield died on September 19. On September 20, Arthur became the twenty-first US president.

1886

On November 18, Chester Arthur died.

Young Chester

Chester Alan Arthur was born in Fairfield, Vermont, on October 5, 1829. He had six sisters and two brothers.

In 1844, the Arthurs moved to Schenectady, New York. There, Chester began college. He was 15 years old. After school, Chester studied law.

★ FAST FACTS ★

Born: October 5, 1829

Wife: Ellen Lewis Herndon (1837–1880)

Children: three

Political Party: Republican

Age at Inauguration: 51

Years Served: 1881–1885

Vice President: None

Died: November 18, 1886, age 57

Chester's mother, Malvina Stone Arthur, was from New Hampshire.

Chester's father, William Arthur, moved to America from Ireland when he was 18.

9

Civil Rights Lawyer

Arthur's father spoke out against slavery. Arthur shared his father's views. In 1853, Arthur began working under **lawyer** Erastus D. Culver. Arthur helped Culver fight for slaves' rights.

In 1852, Jonathan Lemmon and his wife had taken eight slaves from Virginia to New York. New York did not allow slavery. So, the slaves wanted their freedom.

Lemmon refused to free the slaves. Arthur and Culver fought for them in court. The judge granted the slaves their freedom.

Arthur
worked hard,
was smart,
and loved
the law.

11

In 1854, Arthur passed his law tests. He became a **lawyer**. He also became a partner in Culver's law firm.

In 1855, Arthur fought another important case. He **defended** an African-American woman. Her name was Lizzie Jennings.

Jennings had been forced off a New York **streetcar** reserved for white people. Arthur won $500 for Jennings. The win also changed New York laws.

After the case, **discrimination** on New York public **transportation** was not allowed. African Americans could ride any streetcar. Arthur became famous around New York.

After the Jennings case, Arthur became known as a defender of the rights of African Americans.

In 1854, Congress passed the Kansas-Nebraska Act. This act stated that settlers of these territories could decide if they wanted to allow slavery.

Starting a Family

In 1856, Arthur started his own law practice in New York City. Around this time, he met Ellen Lewis Herndon. Ellen was outgoing and loved to sing. Arthur and Ellen married on October 25, 1859.

Arthur and Ellen had three children. William Lewis was born in 1860. Sadly, he died when he was just two. Chester Alan was born in 1864. He was called Alan. In 1871, Ellen Herndon was born. The family called her Nelly.

The Arthur family

Entering Politics

In New York, Arthur grew more interested in **politics**. He helped form the new **Republican** Party. He soon attracted the attention of party leaders.

In 1860, Governor Edwin D. Morgan named Arthur state **engineer**-in-chief. In 1861, the **American Civil War** began. Arthur was in charge of giving supplies to the state's **militia**.

Arthur became the New York quartermaster general in 1861. His duties included providing troops with supplies.

New York Governor Edwin D. Morgan later served in the US Senate, from 1863 to 1869.

Government Work

In 1863, a **Democrat** took over as governor of New York. Morgan and his **staff** lost their jobs. So, Arthur returned to his law practice.

In 1868, Arthur helped Ulysses S. Grant win the presidential election. Grant made Arthur the collector of the New York customhouse. At the time, it was the nation's largest **federal** office.

Arthur hired workers for the customhouse. He gave many key jobs to **Republicans**. In return, they gave money to the Republican Party. This made the party wealthy and powerful.

The *New York Times* said Arthur had done more work to shape the state's Republican Party than anyone else.

Sad Days

In 1877, Rutherford B. Hayes became the nineteenth president. The next year, Arthur lost his job at the customhouse. He returned to practicing law.

Arthur continued be active in the **Republican** Party. He was soon named chairman of the New York Republican Party.

In January 1880, Arthur's wife became ill with **pneumonia**. She died on January 12. Arthur was deeply saddened by the loss of his wife. After her death, Arthur had trouble working.

Ellen Arthur was just 42 years old when she died.

Vice President

In June 1880, the **Republicans** chose James A. Garfield to run for president. Garfield chose Arthur to run for vice president. That November, Arthur and Garfield won the election. They took office on March 4, 1881.

But Garfield did not serve long as president. He was shot on July 2, and struggled to live for months. Garfield died on September 19. The next day, Arthur took the **oath** of office and became president.

Before becoming president, James A. Garfield was Senator-elect. This is an elected Senate member who has not yet been seated.

JAMES A. GARFIELD   CHESTER A. ARTHUR

President Arthur

As president, Arthur improved the US Navy. Because of this, he became known as the "Father of the American Navy."

Then, in 1883, Arthur signed the Pendleton **Civil Service** Act. This act is still in effect today. It requires the **federal** government to hire people based on ability, not **political** party.

Unfortunately, about one year after he became president, Arthur

SUPREME COURT APPOINTMENTS

Horace Gray: 1882

Samuel Blatchford: 1882

PRESIDENT ARTHUR'S CABINET

September 20, 1881–March 4, 1885

★ **STATE:** James G. Blaine,
   Frederick T. Frelinghuysen (from
   December 19, 1881)

★ **TREASURY:** William Windom,
   Charles J. Folger (from November 14, 1881),
   Walter Q. Gresham (from September 24,
   1884),
   Hugh McCulloch (from October 31, 1884)

★ **WAR:** Robert Todd Lincoln

★ **NAVY:** William Henry Hunt,
   William Eaton Chandler (from April 17, 1882)

★ **ATTORNEY GENERAL:** Wayne MacVeagh,
   Benjamin H. Brewster (from January 3,
   1882)

★ **INTERIOR:** Samuel Jordan Kirkwood,
   Henry M. Teller (from April 17, 1882)

25

learned he was ill. His kidneys weren't working correctly. He had Bright's disease.

Arthur kept his illness a secret. He did not want people to think he was too sick to lead the nation. He took vacations so he could rest.

Despite his illness, Arthur loved to have dances and fancy dinners at the White House. When friends and dinner guests left, Arthur often worked late into the night.

Every year, President Arthur's popularity grew. However, some of his ideas were not what the **Republicans** wanted. They did not choose him to run for president in the 1884 election.

In summer 1883, Arthur (*left*) traveled to Yellowstone National Park. He enjoyed the outdoors and spent much time fishing.

Arthur Goes Home

Arthur accepted the party's decision. He knew he was too sick to be president again. After finishing his term, Arthur went home to New York.

Back in New York, Arthur returned to his law practice. But he lacked the **energy** to work. On November 18, 1886, Chester Arthur died.

Arthur will always be remembered as an honest man. He fought for the rights of all people. He worked hard to prove he could be a good leader for America.

Arthur was just 57 years old when he died. He is buried in Rural Cemetery in Albany, New York.

Office of the President

Branches of Government

The US government has three branches. They are the executive, legislative, and judicial branches. Each branch has some power over the others. This is called a system of checks and balances.

★ **Executive Branch**

The executive branch enforces laws. It is made up of the president, the vice president, and the president's cabinet. The president represents the United States around the world. He or she also signs bills into law and leads the military.

★ **Legislative Branch**

The legislative branch makes laws, maintains the military, and regulates trade. It also has the power to declare war. This branch includes the Senate and the House of Representatives. Together, these two houses form Congress.

★ **Judicial Branch**

The judicial branch interprets laws. It is made up of district courts, courts of appeals, and the Supreme Court. District courts try cases. Sometimes people disagree with a trial's outcome. Then he or she may appeal. If a court of appeals supports the ruling, a person may appeal to the Supreme Court.

Qualifications for Office

To be president, a candidate must be at least 35 years old. The person must be a natural-born US citizen. He or she must also have lived in the United States for at least 14 years.

Electoral College

The US presidential election is an indirect election. Voters from each state choose electors. These electors represent their state in the Electoral College. Each elector has one electoral vote. Electors cast their vote for the candidate with the highest number of votes from people in their state. A candidate must receive the majority of Electoral College votes to win.

Term of Office

Each president may be elected to two four-year terms. The presidential election is held on the Tuesday after the first Monday in November. The president is sworn in on January 20 of the following year. At that time, he or she takes the oath of office.
It states:

> I do solemnly swear (or affirm) that I will faithfully execute the office of President of the United States, and will to the best of my ability, preserve, protect and defend the Constitution of the United States.

Line of Succession

The Presidential Succession Act of 1947 states who becomes president if the president cannot serve. The vice president is first in the line. Next are the Speaker of the House and the President Pro Tempore of the Senate. It may happen that none of these individuals is able to serve. Then the office falls to the president's cabinet members. They would take office in the order in which each department was created:

Secretary of State

Secretary of the Treasury

Secretary of Defense

Attorney General

Secretary of the Interior

Secretary of Agriculture

Secretary of Commerce

Secretary of Labor

Secretary of Health and Human Services

Secretary of Housing and Urban Development

Secretary of Transportation

Secretary of Energy

Secretary of Education

Secretary of Veterans Affairs

Secretary of Homeland Security

Benefits

★ While in office, the president receives a salary. It is $400,000 per year. He or she lives in the White House. The president also has 24-hour Secret Service protection.

★ The president may travel on a Boeing 747 jet. This special jet is called Air Force One. It can hold 70 passengers. It has kitchens, a dining room, sleeping areas, and more. Air Force One can fly halfway around the world before needing to refuel. It can even refuel in flight!

★ When the president travels by car, he or she uses Cadillac One. It is a Cadillac Deville that has been modified. The car has heavy armor and communications systems. The president may even take Cadillac One along when visiting other countries.

★ The president also travels on a helicopter. It is called Marine One. It may also be taken along when the president visits other countries.

★ Sometimes the president needs to get away with family and friends. Camp David is the official presidential retreat. It is located in Maryland. The US Navy maintains the retreat. The US Marine Corps keeps it secure. The camp offers swimming, tennis, golf, and hiking.

★ When the president leaves office, he or she receives lifetime Secret Service protection. He or she also receives a yearly pension of $203,700. The former president also receives money for office space, supplies, and staff.

PRESIDENTS AND THEIR TERMS

PRESIDENT	PARTY	TOOK OFFICE	LEFT OFFICE	TERMS SERVED	VICE PRESIDENT
George Washington	None	April 30, 1789	March 4, 1797	Two	John Adams
John Adams	Federalist	March 4, 1797	March 4, 1801	One	Thomas Jefferson
Thomas Jefferson	Democratic-Republican	March 4, 1801	March 4, 1809	Two	Aaron Burr, George Clinton
James Madison	Democratic-Republican	March 4, 1809	March 4, 1817	Two	George Clinton, Elbridge Gerry
James Monroe	Democratic-Republican	March 4, 1817	March 4, 1825	Two	Daniel D. Tompkins
John Quincy Adams	Democratic-Republican	March 4, 1825	March 4, 1829	One	John C. Calhoun
Andrew Jackson	Democrat	March 4, 1829	March 4, 1837	Two	John C. Calhoun, Martin Van Buren
Martin Van Buren	Democrat	March 4, 1837	March 4, 1841	One	Richard M. Johnson
William H. Harrison	Whig	March 4, 1841	April 4, 1841	Died During First Term	John Tyler
John Tyler	Whig	April 6, 1841	March 4, 1845	Completed Harrison's Term	Office Vacant
James K. Polk	Democrat	March 4, 1845	March 4, 1849	One	George M. Dallas
Zachary Taylor	Whig	March 5, 1849	July 9, 1850	Died During First Term	Millard Fillmore

PRESIDENT	PARTY	TOOK OFFICE	LEFT OFFICE	TERMS SERVED	VICE PRESIDENT
Millard Fillmore	Whig	July 10, 1850	March 4, 1853	Completed Taylor's Term	Office Vacant
Franklin Pierce	Democrat	March 4, 1853	March 4, 1857	One	William R.D. King
James Buchanan	Democrat	March 4, 1857	March 4, 1861	One	John C. Breckinridge
Abraham Lincoln	Republican	March 4, 1861	April 15, 1865	Served One Term, Died During Second Term	Hannibal Hamlin, Andrew Johnson
Andrew Johnson	Democrat	April 15, 1865	March 4, 1869	Completed Lincoln's Second Term	Office Vacant
Ulysses S. Grant	Republican	March 4, 1869	March 4, 1877	Two	Schuyler Colfax, Henry Wilson
Rutherford B. Hayes	Republican	March 3, 1877	March 4, 1881	One	William A. Wheeler
James A. Garfield	Republican	March 4, 1881	September 19, 1881	Died During First Term	Chester Arthur
Chester Arthur	Republican	September 20, 1881	March 4, 1885	Completed Garfield's Term	Office Vacant
Grover Cleveland	Democrat	March 4, 1885	March 4, 1889	One	Thomas A. Hendricks
Benjamin Harrison	Republican	March 4, 1889	March 4, 1893	One	Levi P. Morton
Grover Cleveland	Democrat	March 4, 1893	March 4, 1897	One	Adlai E. Stevenson
William McKinley	Republican	March 4, 1897	September 14, 1901	Served One Term, Died During Second Term	Garret A. Hobart, Theodore Roosevelt

PRESIDENT	PARTY	TOOK OFFICE	LEFT OFFICE	TERMS SERVED	VICE PRESIDENT
Theodore Roosevelt	Republican	September 14, 1901	March 4, 1909	Completed McKinley's Second Term, Served One Term	Office Vacant, Charles Fairbanks
William Taft	Republican	March 4, 1909	March 4, 1913	One	James S. Sherman
Woodrow Wilson	Democrat	March 4, 1913	March 4, 1921	Two	Thomas R. Marshall
Warren G. Harding	Republican	March 4, 1921	August 2, 1923	Died During First Term	Calvin Coolidge
Calvin Coolidge	Republican	August 3, 1923	March 4, 1929	Completed Harding's Term, Served One Term	Office Vacant, Charles Dawes
Herbert Hoover	Republican	March 4, 1929	March 4, 1933	One	Charles Curtis
Franklin D. Roosevelt	Democrat	March 4, 1933	April 12, 1945	Served Three Terms, Died During Fourth Term	John Nance Garner, Henry A. Wallace, Harry S. Truman
Harry S. Truman	Democrat	April 12, 1945	January 20, 1953	Completed Roosevelt's Fourth Term, Served One Term	Office Vacant, Alben Barkley
Dwight D. Eisenhower	Republican	January 20, 1953	January 20, 1961	Two	Richard Nixon
John F. Kennedy	Democrat	January 20, 1961	November 22, 1963	Died During First Term	Lyndon B. Johnson
Lyndon B. Johnson	Democrat	November 22, 1963	January 20, 1969	Completed Kennedy's Term, Served One Term	Office Vacant, Hubert H. Humphrey
Richard Nixon	Republican	January 20, 1969	August 9, 1974	Completed First Term, Resigned During Second Term	Spiro T. Agnew, Gerald Ford

PRESIDENT	PARTY	TOOK OFFICE	LEFT OFFICE	TERMS SERVED	VICE PRESIDENT
Gerald Ford	Republican	August 9, 1974	January 20, 1977	Completed Nixon's Second Term	Nelson A. Rockefeller
Jimmy Carter	Democrat	January 20, 1977	January 20, 1981	One	Walter Mondale
Ronald Reagan	Republican	January 20, 1981	January 20, 1989	Two	George H.W. Bush
George H.W. Bush	Republican	January 20, 1989	January 20, 1993	One	Dan Quayle
Bill Clinton	Democrat	January 20, 1993	January 20, 2001	Two	Al Gore
George W. Bush	Republican	January 20, 2001	January 20, 2009	Two	Dick Cheney
Barack Obama	Democrat	January 20, 2009	January 20, 2017	Two	Joe Biden

"Men may die, but the fabrics of our free institutions remain unshaken."

Chester Arthur

★ WRITE TO THE PRESIDENT ★

You may write to the president at:
The White House
1600 Pennsylvania Avenue NW
Washington, DC 20500

You may e-mail the president at:
comments@whitehouse.gov

37

Glossary

American Civil War—the war between the Northern and Southern states from 1861 to 1865.

civil service—the part of the government that is responsible for matters not covered by the military, the courts, or the law.

defend—to speak or write in support of someone or something that is being challenged.

Democrat—a member of the Democratic political party.

discrimination—the treating of some people better than others without any fair or proper reason.

energy (EH-nuhr-jee)—the power or ability to do things.

engineer (ehn-juh-NIHR)—a person who is trained to apply scientific knowledge to a practical purpose such as building machines or buildings.

federal—of or relating to the central government of the United States.

lawyer (LAW-yuhr)—a person who gives people advice on laws or represents them in court.

militia (muh-LIH-shuh)—people who help the army in times of need, they are not soldiers.

oath—a formal promise or statement.

pneumonia—a serious disease that affects the lungs and makes it difficult to breathe.

politics—the art or science of government. Something referring to politics is political. A person who is active in politics is a politician.

Republican—a member of the Republican political party.

staff—a group of people who work for a person or place.

streetcar—a vehicle that travels on streets on metal tracks and that is used for carrying passengers.

transportation—the act of moving people or things from one place to another.

★ WEBSITES ★

To learn more about the US Presidents, visit **booklinks.abdopublishing.com**. These links are routinely monitored and updated to provide the most current information available.

Index